# WOW! Women of Destiny Devotional: 21 Days To Destiny Challenge

WOW! Women of Destiny Devotional
# 21 Days To Destiny Challenge
21 Day Journey of Creating A Life Full Of Passion, Purpose, And Power Designed To Inspire and Refresh Women

EARMA BROWN
PINK TREE PUBLISHING

WOW! Women of Destiny Devotional
21 Days To Destiny Challenge

© Copyright 2016 WOW! Women of Destiny Devotional: 21 Days To Destiny Challenge. Earma Brown. All rights reserved. No part of this book may be reproduced, stored in a retrieval system, or transmitted by any means, electronic, mechanical, photocopying, recording, or otherwise, without written permission from the author, except for the inclusion of brief quotations in a review.

**Published in the United States of America**

Unless otherwise indicated, all Scripture quotations are taken from the Holy Bible: New International Version, Copyright © 1983 by the B.B. Kirkbridge Bible Company, Inc. and The Zondervan Corporation, Grand Rapids, Michigan. Verses marked TLB are taken from The Living Bible, © 1971 by Tyndale House Publishers. Verses marked AMP are taken from The Amplified Bible, © 1965 by Zondervan Publishing House. Verses marked KJV are taken from the King James Version Bible, © 2000 by The Zondervan Corporation.

# Dedication

This book is dedicated to Linda Howard. She is a WOW!
Woman and my dear sister.

# Preface

Welcome to the *WOW! Women of Destiny Devotional - 21 Days To Destiny Challenge,* an important tool written to inspire and refresh the WOW! Women of Destiny readers. The devotionals reinforce the spiritual precepts presented in the *WOW! Women* book series, especially the Women of Destiny.

Thank you for taking the 21 Days To Destiny Challenge! I'm excited for the journey you are embarking on in the Word of God. The twenty-one devotionals start in the next few pages.

I encourage you to take a focus in this challenge. What would you like to see God do in your life? I purposely keep the devotionals simple. Our Scripture focus is one scripture (the same one for the entire twenty-one days). And the confession is one phrase with a blank space for your focus or whatever the Holy Spirit gives you to put there.

### 21 Days To Destiny Challenge Exercise:

- Memorize Memory Scripture, Pray and Say it aloud throughout every day of the challenge.
- Memory Scripture: But the good woman—what a different story! For the good woman—the blameless, the upright, the woman of peace—she has a wonderful future ahead for her. For her there is a happy ending. –Psalms 37:37
- Scripture Confession: I am a woman of destiny, prepared to do God's good works. _____.

May I pray over you?

Father, I ask that you bless each person taking this challenge. Father bless them according to what they need. Encourage, strengthen, deliver, set free, heal through Your Word. Holy Spirit we invite your presence. Speak to God's people. Have your way. Do what only you can do. In Jesus Name, I pray. Amen!

**Now for how the W.O.R.D. Challenge works:**

The Holy Spirit has been guiding me through Biblical and Rhema Word challenges for years. He would speak a certain word, phrase or biblical passage. I would do a word study and discover a whole new conversation with God. I write down whatever He gives me. Then I pray over it, meditate on it, act on it as opportunity arises. As an example, I've been meditating on this Scripture passage: He fills my life with good things so that my youth is renewed like the eagle's. -Psalm 103:5

But this time, I felt prompted to invite you and some of the groups I influence. So, I'm starting with the WOW Women Global group members.

Inside the challenge, you'll receive a devotional each day. We will pray the word, act on the word and expect to receive answered prayer, changed hearts and lives. The acronym W.O.R.D. stands for wisdom, opportunity, revelation and demand.

**Wisdom.** We pray for God's wisdom and blessing as we seek to renew and transform our minds according to Romans 12:1.

**Opportunity.** Like the seed to the sower, God's word will not return void. But it will accomplish what it has been sent to do.

**Revelation.** We can expect God himself to be revealed to us through His Holy Spirit, His Word, His Names and His Son, Jesus.

**Demand.** We become doers of God's word and not only hearers as we apply it to our life. Many times in the Gospels, Jesus was found saying to someone, "Your faith has made you whole! Your faith has done it. Receive your miracle!" So in the same way, in this challenge we are preparing our hearts to receive thereby placing a demand on our faith. We can expect to ask and receive; seek and find; knock and it be opened unto us.

One more thing, anytime you see change, breakthrough or answered prayer in any form during or after the 21 Days To Destiny Challenge testify. Post a comment on 21 Days To Destiny Challenge page or the testimonial page at the website http://www.wowontheweb.com Remember, we overcome by the Blood of the Lamb and the word of our testimony.

*In Service to Christ,*
*Earma Brown*

## Table of Contents

**Dedication 5**

**Preface 7**

**Day 1: A Woman's Destiny 13**

**Day 2: Your Destiny-ation! 15**

**Day 3: Run The Race Well 17**

**Day 4: Pursue His Presence 19**

**Day 5: TRUST God's Process 21**

**Day 6: Six Darts To Divide 25**

**Day 7: Seize The Season 29**

**Day 8: Spirit Of Readiness 31**

**Day 9: Spirit Of Readi…, 2 33**

**Day 10: Lit For A Purpose 35**

**Day 11: The Light Of Fame 37**

**Day 12: Enemies of Destiny 39**

**Day 13: Your Purpose 41**

**Day 14: The Precocious 43**

**Day 15: Enemy To Purpose 45**

**Day 16: Prayer Power 47**

**Day 17: Grow In God 49**

**Day 18: The Divine Yes 51**

**Day 19: Powers Of Destiny 53**

**Day 20: Decide And Act 55**

**Day 21: Driving Force To Continue 57**

**About Author 61**

**Join the WOW! Women Movement! 63**

**Notes: 69**

**Notes: 70**

**Notes: 71**

**Notes: 72**

**Notes: 73**

# Day 1: A Woman's Destiny

*WOW Word of the Day: But the good woman—what a different story! For the good woman—the blameless, the upright, the woman of peace—she has a wonderful future ahead for her. For her there is a happy ending. –Psalms 37:37 TLB*

Have you wondered why the Cinderella story and others like it has such a timeless appeal to many? It's because Father God has put in each of us a desire, a dream, a hope for a bright future and a happy ending. It touches the deep-seated hunger to be and do what we have been destined for.

God has made arrangements to satisfy that hunger in us. He has planned our bright future and happy ending. The prophet Jeremiah proclaiming God's heart said, "I know the plans I have for you; plans of good and not evil, to give you a hope and future."

To expand our understanding of God's thoughts toward us, let's examine some terms used in the Scripture above. The word plan is defined as thoughts, blueprint, direction or purpose.

Hope is your expectancy of good, your dream, an expected end and even your purpose or destination. In addition, future is explained as your chance to succeed, your due season, your final outcome, your fate or simply destiny. (Webster's New World Dictionary and Thesaurus)

Let's take another look at what God said through the prophet Jeremiah using some of the definitive words above, "For I know the (thoughts, blueprint, direction or purpose) that I have for you, saith the Lord, a (purpose) of peace and not evil, to give you (your expectancy of good, your dream, an expected end) and (your chance to succeed, your due season or destiny.)"

You see God has planted our dreams of good fortune and having a happy ending within us in seed form. Within each seed is the blueprint of our individual destiny, an expected end and even our bright future. Join me as we uncover the Biblical principles of developing the seeds of destiny given to each of us.

**21 Days To Destiny Challenge Exercise** (Memorize Memory Scripture, Pray and Say it aloud throughout every day of the challenge.)

**Memory Scripture:** For we are God's workmanship, created in Christ Jesus to do good works, which God prepared in advance for us to do. (Eph. 2:10).

**Confession:** I am a woman of destiny, prepared in advance to do good works

_____

_____

_____

# Day 2: Your Destiny-ation!

WOW Word for the Day: *But He, being compassionate, forgave their iniquity and did not destroy them; And often He restrained His anger And did not arouse all His wrath. Thus He remembered that they were but flesh, A wind that passes and does not return. Psalms 78:38, 39*

Realize the brevity of life. The Ecclesiastes writer describes our lives here on earth as a shuttle traveling swiftly through time. Learn to number your days correctly. Jesus said to his disciples and now to us, "The day is almost ended, we must quickly fulfill our God-given task for night is coming, when no man can work."

With that said, the time is now to pursue, discover and fulfill our destiny, our appointed purpose here on earth. In this book, I've outlined seven steps to take in discovering your destiny. They helped me connect and find my destiny. I hope they will do the same for you.

1. Pursue God's presence. Let him give you His perspective. Ask God for His wisdom. All through the Bible inspired writers claim wisdom is the principal thing. Then listen a lot and pray more.

2. Embrace the power of preparation. Knowing the power of preparation will keep you going through mistakes and fumbled decisions of life. This knowledge will cause you to view failure in a perspective that will cause you to get up and be strengthened instead of destroyed. You won't give in to languishing in self-pity. You will get up; brush yourself off and go at it again.

3.Seizing the season. Recognize 'Now is the time. The main principle of gaining a sense of destiny is realizing that our time here on earth is brief. My prayer has become that of the Psalmist when he said, "Teach us to number our days and recognize how few they are; help us to spend them as we should. –Psalms 91:12

4.Stir the fires of your passion. Raise your level of intensity. Stir up the gifts that lay within you to be used for God's glory. When you put these principles into action, you will learn how to truly turn the lemons of life into lemonade. You'll take those glasses of lemonade and serve them to the world.

5.Discover your God-given individual purpose. Find out what God put you on the earth to do. If you don't know, just ask. Ask and receive. Use God's phone number Jer. 33:3 Call unto me and I will show you great and mighty things…Then identify what seeks to make you ineffective.

6.Experience the power of fulfilling your destiny. Know your future, your destiny is stored in your heart. It's not dictated by your past or present circumstances.

7.Run with perseverance the race that is marked out for you. Be patient with yourself and others as you walk out the will and purpose of God.

Finally, let us leave a legacy of mentorship. Are you preparing your life as a torch to pass on?

**21 Days To Destiny Challenge Exercise** (Memorize Memory Scripture, Pray and Say it aloud throughout every day of the challenge.)

**Memory Scripture:** For we are God's workmanship, created in Christ Jesus to do good works, which God prepared in advance for us to do. (Eph. 2:10).

**Confession:** I am a woman of destiny, prepared in advance to do good works

_____

_____

_____

_____

# Day 3: Run The Race Well

*WOW Word of the Day: Teach us to number our days and recognize how few they are; help us to spend them as we should. –Psalms 91:12.*

I discovered that in any contest for a prize there will be obstacles—things that will rise up to hinder or resist you in your contest. Therefore, it's no surprise it's the same with life in general.

Interruptions, distractions, obstacles may seek to stop us from receiving our prize (happy life, good and expected ending, heavenly home) But God has not left us to fight alone. What are some of the things that we should lay aside that may hinder us in our race of life?

Half-heartedness. Do you not know that those who run in a race all runs but one receives the prize? Therefore, run in such a way that you may obtain it.

Complacency. Que se ra, se ra…You know whatever will be, will be. Don't just lean back and accept whatever comes to you. Take life by the wheel and go after what you want.

Prayerlessness. You have not because you ask not. Jesus reminded us in the Gospels that, "Man ought to always pray and not give up."

Impatience. Quickly giving up. The Ecclesiastes writer supports this principle by saying the race is not given to the swift nor the skilled but the who perseveres.

Sin. Sin will stop us in our tracks, if we allow it. Our Lord Jesus has paid a great price for the opportunity we have to repent and make it right. Before His death, burial and resurrection we had a faulty access to the Father. Now, we can go boldly to His throne through Jesus and ask for forgiveness and receive it. So, don't let sin block your blessed life and your happy ending. Repent, receive and rejoice in the race!

You see God has lovingly arranged and designed your future. Has it emerged like a shining sun in your heart, yet? If not already, I pray it will soon. He, our Father, has arranged beforehand that we each would have our chance to succeed in the race of life. So take the advice offered from your cloud of witnesses, run your race well! Remember, we have a choice and a responsibility to lay aside every weight and the sin that so easily ensnares us.

**21 Days To Destiny Challenge Exercise** (Memorize Memory Scripture, Pray and Say it aloud throughout every day of the challenge.)

**Memory Scripture:** For we are God's workmanship, created in Christ Jesus to do good works, which God prepared in advance for us to do. (Eph. 2:10).

**Confession:** I am a woman of destiny, prepared in advance to do good works.

_____

_____

_____

# Day 4: Pursue His Presence

*WOW Word for Today: Seek continually. Seek the Lord and his strength, seek his face continually –I Chronicles 16:11*

Have you felt disqualified from destiny because of your past? Rahab may have felt that way. She is a wonderful trophy of God's grace and merciful intent. Yet, she didn't start out that way. As you may know, her past included prostitution. She pushed past her feelings of disqualifications and made a declaration, "Your God is God." The first step toward realizing the destiny for God's woman is her pursuit of God's presence. I call it pursuing God's presence and not so much the gift. Five suggestions to pursuing the presence of God:

Seek first the Kingdom of God. The Kingdom of God is not meat and drink nor the body. But is peace, joy, love and other fruits of the Spirit. Don't seek your destiny, seek Him and you will find your destiny (His desired end).

Seek Him with all your heart. He has promised when we seek him with a whole heart we will surely find him.

Seek humbly. The Psalmist writer encourages us with, "The Lord is good and glad to teach the proper path to all who go astray; he will teach the ways that are right and best to those who humbly turn to him…Where is the man who fears the Lord? God will teach him how to choose the best (Psalm

25:8,9,12). In other words, seek God humbly and he will teach you how to choose your destiny.

Seek Him through meditating on God's Word. In defining the word meditation, we can see more clearly how to meditate on God's Word. Meditation means to ponder, think about a lot, and mutter under your breath. In the first book of Joshua, God instructs Joshua (now us) how to have good success in everything he does. He says to meditate on His word day and night. So, it becomes clear to have good success, we will think about, ponder and mutter under our breath.

Seek continually. Seek the Lord and his strength, seek his face continually (I Chronicles 16:11). The Physician Luke admonishes us to, "Keep on asking and you will keep on getting; keep on looking and you will keep on finding; knock and the door will be opened. Everyone who asks, receives; all who seek, find; and the door is opened to everyone who knocks (Luke 11:9-10).

After accepting our Lord's death as sufficient, we must turn and freely give what was freely given to us. Walk in forgiveness. Remember, forgiveness is not a feeling but a choice. So join me as I purpose anew to walk in the power of forgiveness by faith.

**21 Days To Destiny Challenge Exercise** (Memorize Memory Scripture, Pray and Say it aloud throughout every day of the challenge.)

**Memory Scripture:** For we are God's workmanship, created in Christ Jesus to do good works, which God prepared in advance for us to do. (Eph. 2:10).

**Confession:** I am a woman of destiny, prepared in advance to do good works.

_____

_____

_____

# Day 5: TRUST God's Process

*WOW Word for Today: By faith, the Israelites marched around the walls of Jericho for seven days, and the walls fell flat. 31 By an act of faith, Rahab, the Jericho harlot, welcomed the spies and escaped the destruction that came on those who <u>refused to trust God</u>.*

Have you been asking God for a whale (big fish of a promise)? I know I have. If so, don't be surprised when He moves you out of the little pond (comfortable place), to enlarge your capacity to receive. Perhaps it's no news to you; I've discovered He cannot send a whale to our little pond.

So, guess what, we have to change. We have to change our mind, our heart and sometimes our place, position and perspective must change. I hear you that can be a lot of changing. But remember we are being changed to a better place.

For example, some of you (us) have been praying, Lord take me to the next level, increase me, bless me, enlarge my territory and even give me my destiny, right? Which, as you know, are not bad requests. The Word of God says our Father takes us from glory to glory and He wants to increase us, bless us, enlarge us and even gives us our destiny (bright future, our expected end.)

Here's the problem sometimes in response to our prayers change happens; then we get all confused. We start doubting ourselves and God's plan. God I prayed for increase. Why did I lose my job? I prayed that you enlarge me and now I'm in a battle. Consider this, God may be moving you from the little pond to the sea or even the ocean. Remember, whales don't swim in little ponds.

Whatever it takes, know that the longer your process, the bigger the promise (next level) is going to be. God does not cut corners or waste our pain. He works all things to our good. (Romans 8:28)

Let me be clear Father God is faithful. He will not fail us or forsake us. So here is our pattern to follow, we must submit to the process. Here are some suggestions formed into the acronym T.R.U.S.T. that will help us through the process.

Timing. First of all, God's plan and timing is always perfect. (Ecclesiastes 3) Ours is not. It takes time to walk through the process. If we try to depend on just our sense of when things should be done, we may miss God. If we pray and ask for His timing, we will have success. Operating in God's timing, we may have to wait and others times we must act when He says act.

Recompense: God will recompense. He always recompenses. The first time I heard the word recompense, I knew it was God speaking because that word was not in my vocabulary. If you hear nothing else I say, get this one in your spirit. Jehovah Gmolah is one of the names of God. Whatever losses you experience in the process, you can expect Father God will pay you back. He will restore.

Understanding. It's our human nature or fleshy nature, that we feel we have to always understand everything intellectually. It may not be to our best interest to know everything.

Sovereign: God is in control. Say yes to His will. Acknowledge God is still God, even if we don't understand everything at the moment. Believe He has something bigger and better in mind. This is where the element of trust enters, if we allow it. God is sovereign.

Territory: After God has moved you from your little pond, know that you are at the brink of your promise, your increase, your new level. But it's not time to relax; it's time to get ready to rumble (fight.) Not the way we're used to fighting. Get full of God's Word and fight the way He fights, by the Spirit. (2 Cor. 10:4) Pray more; listen more.

Get your plans, your strategies from God. He'll take you by the hand and help you. There are times you won't have to fight for the battle is the Lord's.

There are other times you must fight the good fight of faith, using weapons that are not carnal but mighty to the pulling down of strongholds. (2 Cor. 10:4)

So, keep praying to God to bless you, increase you and enlarge your territory. He will. It's his good pleasure to do so. Just be ready for the conquest, taking dominion and occupying the good land he's given you. It takes pressure and sometimes pain to get you to the next level and into your destiny. Don't be dismayed and confused about what you're going through. Ultimately, Jesus has given us the victory. The writer to the Corinthians said it like this, "Now thanks be to God who always leads us in triumph in Christ... (2 Corinthians 2:14) T.R.U.S.T God and know that He is in control. Listen to Him, follow Him, submit to the process and He'll get you to your destiny-ation, safely.

**21 Days To Destiny Challenge Exercise** (Memorize Memory Scripture, Pray and Say it aloud throughout every day of the challenge.)

**Memory Scripture:** For we are God's workmanship, created in Christ Jesus to do good works, which God prepared in advance for us to do. (Eph. 2:10).

**Confession:** I am a woman of destiny, prepared in advance to do good works.

_____

_____

_____

# Day 6: Six Darts To Divide

*WOW Words of Today: Blessed are the pure in heart for they shall see God.*

Jesus said, "Blessed are the pure in heart for they shall see God. To see God is to be an intimate friend. There's a scripture that says, "Friendship of God is reserved for those who reverence the Lord."

Pride is an enemy of intimacy with God. Back in the Garden of Eden, when Adam and Eve failed God and sin broke their fellowship. I suspect that was one of the things that hurt the most, their loss of intimacy with Father God. The couple knew no resistance until the event of their sin. The Bible plainly tells us God resists the proud.

Duplicity is a divided heart. Let no double minded man think he will receive anything from God. A double mind with the things of God will always hinder us. Many times, lack of focus boils down to a double mind. When I catch myself with a divided focus toward the destiny of God, I'll stop, repent and ask the Holy Spirit for right focus.

Wrong motives work against our relationship with God. A past jail ministry leader would always say about the inmates we were inviting to come to a church service our group hosted every Thursday night in a halfway house for men, don't worry about them coming with wrong motives. We've all had wrong motives (doing the right thing for the wrong reason) at one time or another. Perhaps they are coming to look at the pretty girls on our team. The fact is when they get in the church service atmosphere with worship, the Holy Spirit can work with them and convict them of any sin and wrong motives. As He does with us all; he works with us to change our heart and motives (intentions).

Disorganization can give place to the enemy; for he thrives in disorder. God is a god of order. Just like in the little story I began, if we're there, steeped in clutter and disorganization and don't know how to get out of this pattern, you're in a good place. You know you need help and you know who can fix it. Practically, start with the small. Do that to completion. Then do the next step God shows you. How do I know? It's all started and finished in faith. Just do it and see what happens.

Worldly distractions can take many forms. Distractions can be anything good or bad that moves your attention away from the great that God has called us to do. Make sure your television time is not luring your heart away from God. I know this is not a popular topic but I must say this. Your seemingly innocent entertainment via T.V. shows with worldly values and agendas may become distractions and corrupt the good character you've built in your life. Simply put, remember bad company corrupts good character.

Fleshly. The Bible says the flesh is at enmity with God. If we allow the flesh to rule in our life, we eventually open the door to the enemy. By the flesh, I mean the natural man that wants to do everything it wants to do and at any time it wants to do it. For example, your old nature you may choose to live an undisciplined life.

There's only one thing left to say, start small and start now. Father God will meet you wherever you are. It's a good thing, he doesn't require us to clean up ourselves and straighten up our mess before we come to Jesus. You can come to God just as you are. Let Jesus be Lord of your life, as well as, Savior.

**21 Days To Destiny Challenge Exercise** (Memorize Memory Scripture, Pray and Say it aloud throughout every day of the challenge.)

**Memory Scripture:** For we are God's workmanship, created in Christ Jesus to do good works, which God prepared in advance for us to do. (Eph. 2:10).

**Confession:** I am a woman of destiny, prepared in advance to do good works.

_____

_____

_____

# Day 7: Seize The Season

*WOW Words of Today: There is a season for every activity under heaven. –Eccl. 3:1b*

Do you know what season your life is in? Are you in the preparation season? Or are you living your dream and destiny? For many the preparation season is spent preparing for a destiny to come.

For others, it might be going through the process. God has communicated to you; the next level or the promise is coming. You might know by now, that means the process is about to happen which readies you for the next level. For He only shows a few steps of the staircase at a time.

Whatever season, this message finds you in, you should maximize it. Live it to the fullest. Many times, over the years, I found myself mourning over a past season or spending too much time wishing for the next season. Instead, I've learned to live fully in my present season, yet remain expectant for the upcoming season.

The word maximize means to assign maximum importance to; to find a maximum value of; the period of highest, greatest or utmost development (plain terms: to give the best of all that you have to God and to receive all that God has for you in your present season.)

Recognize and know your season. There really is a season for everything. The wise writer of Ecclesiastes 3:1 There is a time for everything, and a season for every activity under heaven.

Decide to use your gifts and talents for God's glory. Make your calling and election sure. Matthew 25:14-30; 2 Peter 1:3-10

Live a balanced life. Live ready. Ready for what? Ready for God's purpose and plan to come forth in your life. Ready for the fulfillment of God's Word in your life. Ready for God's opportunities. Ready to connect with your destiny. Ready to be about our Father's business. Ready for the Second Coming of our Lord! I Timothy 4:2 Preach the Word; be ready in season and out of season; reprove, rebuke, exhort, with great patience and instruction. Matthew 25:1-13 Parable of Ten Virgins

Encourage others in their season. Scriptural Reference: Hebrews 10:23, 24, 25 Let us hold unswervingly to the hope we profess, for he who promised is faithful. 24 And let us consider how we may spur one another on toward love and good deeds. 25 Let us not give up meeting together, as some are in the habit of doing, but let us encourage one another—all the more as you see the Day approaching.

With all that said, we know we will experience different seasons at different times in our life. As we stay connected and led by God's Spirit, we can discern and know the seasons of life. In this chapter, we have been discussing our preparation season and how we can operate in a spirit of readiness and stay ready for God's opportunity and destiny.

**21 Days To Destiny Challenge Exercise** (Memorize Memory Scripture, Pray and Say it aloud throughout every day of the challenge.)

**Memory Scripture:** For we are God's workmanship, created in Christ Jesus to do good works, which God prepared in advance for us to do. (Eph. 2:10).

**Confession:** I am a woman of destiny, prepared in advance to do good works.

# Day 8: Spirit Of Readiness

*WOW Words of Today: God is not a man, that He should lie. Nor a son of man, that He should repent. Has He said and will He not do? Or has He spoken and will He not make it good? --Numbers 23:19*

Perhaps, you are in the midst of a change that you never thought would happen. If so, this little word is for you today. I encourage you to call to the one who changes not. Our Father God does not change. In fact, he is the same yesterday, today and forever. He promised he would never leave us or forsake us. And you know what; I believe Him. On that note, I've gathered some Scriptures that I have found comforting and faith building in the middle of CHANGES in my life and all around me.

Blessed be the Lord my Rock, who trains my hands for war, And my fingers for battle--My Lovingkindness and my fortress, My high tower and my deliverer, My Shield and the One in whom I take refuge. --Psalm 144:1,2a

"For I am the Lord, I do not change; --Malachi 3:6a

Let your conduct be without covetousness; be content with such things as you have. For He Himself has said, "I will never leave you nor forsake you." So we may boldly say: "The Lord is my helper; I will not fear. What can man do to me?"

"God is not a man, that He should lie. Nor a son of man, that He should repent. Has He said and will He not do? Or has He spoken and will He not make it good? --Numbers 23:19

**21 Days To Destiny Challenge Exercise** (Memorize Memory Scripture, Pray and Say it aloud throughout every day of the challenge.)

**Memory Scripture:** For we are God's workmanship, created in Christ Jesus to do good works, which God prepared in advance for us to do. (Eph. 2:10).

**Confession:** I am a woman of destiny, prepared in advance to do good works

_____

_____

_____

# Day 9: Spirit Of Readi..., 2

*WOW Words of Today: For ye have need of patience, that, after ye have done the will of God, ye might receive the promise. -Hebrews 10:36*

Prioritize your family, business and life. Make sure God is first, family, work, church and then other stuff. Right priorities will safeguard your life. Most sin happens when something is out of balance with wrong priorities. For example, if you're putting work or church before God and family. Keep right priorities and prosper beyond your wildest dreams.

Learn early to redeem your time. Look for lost time (unredeemed) evenings, early mornings, late nights. In other words, if you're spending all your free time in front of television, you might not connect with your destiny in your life time.

Apply patience. The word of says to exercise patience so that afterwards you may receive the promises of God. Notice there's action inside this instruction. Most people think of patience in the noun or passive form. But, I've discovered it's more of an action, a verb.

Do as Jesus did. Jesus wrapped himself in a towel preparing to serve his disciples and impart the vision of servanthood in their hearts. By allowing Him to serve them, they learned a lesson they would never forget. Write it down.

Embrace your season of preparation. Life really is cyclical. It comes around in season. You may be going through a season where it looks like nothing is happening. It may be your preparation season for the greatness that's coming. Take advantage of it; don't waste it.

**21 Days To Destiny Challenge Exercise** (Memorize Memory Scripture, Pray and Say it aloud throughout every day of the challenge.)

**Memory Scripture:** For we are God's workmanship, created in Christ Jesus to do good works, which God prepared in advance for us to do. (Eph. 2:10).

**Confession:** I am a woman of destiny, prepared in advance to do good works

_____

_____

_____

# Day 10: Lit For A Purpose

*WOW Words of Today: No one lights a lamp and then puts it under a basket. Instead, a lamp is placed on a stand, where it gives light to everyone in the house. -Matthew 5:15*

Have you considered God may have lit your fire for a purpose? Or at the least allowed your fire to be lit. Luke, the physician instructs us, "No one lights a lamp and puts it in a place where it will be hidden." When we received Christ into our heart, we were lit for a purpose. I can only add God will place you where He wills.

Use the power of conviction. Decide to use the power of conviction about the things that get us disturbed. Things that you can absolutely not stand by and watch happen. There's no one else doing anything about it; so you should.

Develop excellence. To develop excellence, aim high. Do your best in all things. Work as unto the Lord. Start habits of excellence.

Set yourself up for success. If you are just beginning, start small. Allow time for the passion curve. The more you fuel your fire, the brighter it will burn.

Stir Enthusiasm. Jump around. Get excited. Make some noise. The more excitement you express, the more contagious you become.

Utilize the slow burn method. Some things take time to manifest. You just have to wait it out. The one who waits for his/her time will be the victor.

**21 Days To Destiny Challenge Exercise** (Memorize Memory Scripture, Pray and Say it aloud throughout every day of the challenge.)

**Memory Scripture:** For we are God's workmanship, created in Christ Jesus to do good works, which God prepared in advance for us to do. (Eph. 2:10).

**Confession:** I am a woman of destiny, prepared in advance to do good works

_____

_____

_____

# Day 11: The Light Of Fame

*WOW Words of Today: You are the light of the world--like a city on a hilltop that cannot be hidden. -Matthew 5:14.*

Did you know our Father God calls us (the Body of Christ) and even gifts us with a measure of fame? One of the greatest powers of fame is influence. He has called us the children of light (Christians) to be an influence for good.

In Scripture, Believers are described as salt and light. Salt preserves, flavors; light illuminates and brings clarity. Both are metaphors of God's call for us to impact and influence our society.

The Apostle Matthew quoting Jesus said it like this, "You are the salt of the earth...You are the light of the world. A city that is set on a hill cannot be hidden. Neither do men light a candle and put it under a bushel, but on a candlestick; and it gives light unto all that are in the house."

He goes on to say, let your light so shine before men that they may see your good works and glorify your Father which is in heaven. (Matthew 5:13a,14-16) Of course, we are all given a measure of fame. (light, influence)

Each measure given is not the same. Just like in the story of the talents, each person was given a different amount. One was given ten, then another five and one was only given one.

As Christians, we are all famous in our area of influence. We are each given a measure of fame (influence) to grow and multiply.

For some of us, we are famous in our family circle or our neighborhood. Others have been given regional or even worldwide fame and influence to spend wisely.

**21 Days To Destiny Challenge Exercise** (Memorize Memory Scripture, Pray and Say it aloud throughout every day of the challenge.)

**Memory Scripture:** For we are God's workmanship, created in Christ Jesus to do good works, which God prepared in advance for us to do. (Eph. 2:10).

**Confession:** I am a woman of destiny, prepared in advance to do good works

_____

_____

_____

# Day 12: Enemies of Destiny

*WOW Words of Today: As Solomon grew old, his wives turned his heart after other gods, and his heart was not fully devoted to the LORD his God, as the heart of David his father had been. -1 King 11:4*

Then, beware of the top six enemies to good influence. I've listed some examples of women in Scripture that failed to use their gifts of influence for good. Each example points to a wrong choice to guard against:

Then, beware of the top six enemies to good influence. I've listed some examples of women in Scripture that failed to use their gifts of influence for good. Each example points to a wrong choice to guard against:

Used her power of invitation to invite husband to sin. Eve, created to be a helper for Adam, invited him to join her in sin. (Gen. 2:18 and 3:6)

Used her power of influence to draw others away from God. Solomon's wives drew his heart away from God. (1 Ki 11:4)

Used her power of enthusiasm. She stirred others to evil action. Jezebel stirred up her husband Ahab to commit acts of abominable wickedness. (1 Kings 21:25)

Used her power of counsel. She gave evil counsel. Job's wife counseled him to "curse God and die." (Job 2:9)

Used her power of persuasion. She convinced or persuaded her husband of an evil plan. Rebekah willfully deceived her husband Isaac. (Genesis 27)

Used her power of encouragement to do the opposite. She despised her husband. Michal despised her husband David. (2 Samuel 6:16)

We as women in Christ are equipped with qualities for good influence. I exhort you to use your gifts to become influencers for Christ through the good you do. Let it be said that by the power of your influence you invited others to Christ, drew some toward God, stirred others to action, gave godly counsel and persuaded many to God's perfect plan.

Let your light of influence be a signal to the weary. Influence others to the good. Godly influencers empower, persuade, and convince others to the reality of Christ and to the common good.

**21 Days To Destiny Challenge Exercise** (Memorize Memory Scripture, Pray and Say it aloud throughout every day of the challenge.)

**Memory Scripture:** For we are God's workmanship, created in Christ Jesus to do good works, which God prepared in advance for us to do. (Eph. 2:10).

**Confession:** I am a woman of destiny, prepared in advance to do good works

_____

_____

_____

# Day 13: Your Purpose

*WOW Word of Today: Whatever you do, do it heartily, as to the Lord and not to men. -Colossians 3:23*

When you receive your purpose from God – your perspective will change: You'll realize God is holding you accountable for what you do with his gifts. Remember Jesus' story of the talents in Matthew 25: 14-30. God gave me a paradigm shift years ago about my talent. I was sitting in a church service listening to a message about the man issuing talents and going on a journey.

The man returns from his journey and discovers the one he issued 5 talents and the one he issued 2 talents doubled their talents. But the one he issued 1 hid his in the ground and did nothing. I heard this story countless times before and nothing happened.

This time was different; conviction from the Holy Spirit came on me and I began to weep. I clearly saw myself as the man with 1 talent who buried his gift. I knew I may as well have literally buried my talent in the ground just like the man for all the good I had done with it.

I prayed, "Father if you give me another chance, I'll develop it, I'll use it and multiply it." That 1 talent was my writing. I'm happy to report to you over twenty years later, with God's help I'm still doing my best to use it and multiply it. In fact, I'm certain my books would never have been born. For sure this article birthed from the books would never have been written if I hadn't prayed that prayer.

Speaking of doing your best, when you receive your appointment God you realize God deserves your best. You'll serve in excellence according to Colossians 3:22-25

22Bondservants, obey in all things your masters according to the flesh, not with eye service, as men-pleasers, but in sincerity of heart, fearing God 23 and whatever you do, do it heartily, as to the Lord and not to men, 24 knowing that from the Lord you will receive the reward of the inheritance for you serve the Lord Christ.

Don't just give God you any old kind of service. Make it your best. Let me mother you a bit, if you're serving in excellence you're going to be on time. If you can't be there – you're going to call and let your authority know what's up and reassure them, you'll be back in place next time. When Varn and I were taking a team of people to the highways and byways to feed the poor, we left at exactly that time. Our team members began to know if they truly wanted to go with us – they had to be on time. Make your service as unto God an excellent gift for His glory.

**21 Days To Destiny Challenge Exercise** (Memorize Memory Scripture, Pray and Say it aloud throughout every day of the challenge.)

**Memory Scripture:** For we are God's workmanship, created in Christ Jesus to do good works, which God prepared in advance for us to do. (Eph. 2:10).

**Confession:** I am a woman of destiny, prepared in advance to do good works

_____

_____

_____

# Day 14: The Precocious

*WOW Word of Today: For we are his workmanship, created in Christ Jesus unto good works, which God hath before ordained that we should walk in them. -Ephesians 2:10.*

You may be like Florence and you received your call at a precocious age. Or you may be like others who received their call later in life. Whichever you may be, now is the time to get connected and fulfil your purpose in life. Are you looking for your God given purpose?

If nothing else, now is the time get started in the direction God's calling you. Here are five little signs to check for hints of your God given purpose along the way:

Check your thought life. What impressions are you getting? What thoughts keep popping up when you're quiet or prayerful? This advice, helped me a lot, in the beginning. My life was so busy with activity that I didn't have much time to look within. But different seasons came, where I had the opportunity to be quiet and examine what I enjoyed thinking about.

Until, those seasons came, I would search for a quiet moment. And I asked God to show me the time. I learned to grab those unredeemed times, we talked about earlier. I found times, like doctor appointments, car wash, kids practice, lunch hour, wee early and way late times when my family was asleep and more. I would make notes.

Those notes would turn into teachings that turned in classes that turned into books that turned into multiple series of books and courses. So, just start.

**21 Days To Destiny Challenge Exercise** (Memorize Memory Scripture, Pray and Say it aloud throughout every day of the challenge.)

**Memory Scripture:** For we are God's workmanship, created in Christ Jesus to do good works, which God prepared in advance for us to do. (Eph. 2:10).

**Confession:** I am a woman of destiny, prepared in advance to do good works

_____

_____

_____

# Day 15: Enemy To Purpose

*WOW Word of Today: Look after each other so that none of you fails to receive the grace of God. Watch out that no poisonous root of bitterness grows up to trouble you, corrupting many. -Hebrews 12:15*

The flesh (our human nature) is one of the greatest enemies to God's purpose in our life. The desire to do it our way, another way, the easy way, the short way or any old way besides God's way strives to dominate. Oh yes, there's the not-at-all pressure which is rooted in rebellion, one of the first mentioned enemies to purpose. Here are four enemies to guard against and protect your purpose:

Bitterness. There are several top things that can turn into bitterness. Unresolved anger and hurt, unforgiveness, traumatic event, hardships are top culprits. Our enemy seeks to take advantage of these things in our lives. We, all at one time or another go through things. And yes, the old saying is true, it's most important how you go through them.

Many of us don't go through, we get stuck. If you suspect, you have a bitter root. First of all, pray and ask the Holy Spirit to help. Give God permission to do what it takes to heal you. Then do the things He suggest one by one. A bitter root, you cannot pull it out yourself. For me, it took courage to confess things, talking with a trusted someone and eventually I went through Christian counseling. If you are in the Dallas area, Jerry and

Jessye Ruffin are a good source for Christian based counseling. Don't overthink it, just obey God's leading.

**21 Days To Destiny Challenge Exercise** (Memorize Memory Scripture, Pray and Say it aloud throughout every day of the challenge.)

**Memory Scripture:** For we are God's workmanship, created in Christ Jesus to do good works, which God prepared in advance for us to do. (Eph. 2:10).

**Confession:** I am a woman of destiny, prepared in advance to do good works

_____

_____

_____

# Day 16: Prayer Power

*WOW Word of Today: But of him are ye in Christ Jesus, who of God is made unto us wisdom, and righteousness, and sanctification, and redemption… -1 Corinthians 1:30.*

Flip Your Perspective. Varn and I delivered a message to a group of servant leaders and armorbearers called the 'Precious Gift Of Impartation.' Within that message, we talked about flipping your wrong perspective to a right perspective.

Let me tell you, if you've ever experienced hardship, persecution or troubling circumstances it's pretty easy to get a wrong perspective. For me back then, we were being persecuted for something we didn't even do in the first place…

Varn turned to me and encouraged me to do what we have been preaching all this time to others, "Flip it." It was time for us to flip our perspective and count precious all the things we had received. It's your time.

Not assuming everyone is going through troubling circumstances but if you are there right now, you have to go through and find the lesson (s) God is wanting you to learn and count them precious. When you can do that, you know that you've successfully flipped it.

**21 Days To Destiny Challenge Exercise** (Memorize Memory Scripture, Pray and Say it aloud throughout every day of the challenge.)

**Memory Scripture:** For we are God's workmanship, created in Christ Jesus to do good works, which God prepared in advance for us to do. (Eph. 2:10).

**Confession:** I am a woman of destiny, prepared in advance to do good works

_____

_____

_____

# Day 17: Grow In God

*WOW Word of Today Therefore, prepare your minds for action; be self-controlled; set your hope fully on the grace to be given you when Jesus Christ is revealed. 1 Peter 1:13*

Grow in self-control. While we are waiting, we have to exercise patience. The more we exercise patience, we grow in self-control. I've discovered our disobedience and rebellion are sometimes birthed out of impatience.

Impatience with what, you might ask. When the wait is long; we get impatient with the plan of God. When we have to wait, it puts the squeeze on our character.

What comes out depends on our maturity and how much we've grown in self-control. So, during your season get control of yourself, exercise some patience and wait. Your promise is on the way.

**21 Days To Destiny Challenge Exercise** (Memorize Memory Scripture, Pray and Say it aloud throughout every day of the challenge.)

**Memory Scripture:** For we are God's workmanship, created in Christ Jesus to do good works, which God prepared in advance for us to do. (Eph. 2:10).

**Confession:** I am a woman of destiny, prepared in advance to do good works

# Day 18: The Divine Yes

*WOW Word of Today: Faith is a lifestyle not a one act deed.5 Strive to be diligent in your faith. We learn about God, His love, His acceptance, His ways, His righteousness, His Word—then we ultimately decide to believe or not believe. -Earma*

Years ago, my then pastor asked me to stand up in a church service to receive a word of prophecy. His words were, "God says he's going to settle you. No more will you be tossed about. No more will you move with uncertainty. I'm settling you starting from the inside out. Like Me, your yes will be yes and your no will be no..."

I can testify God has done this in my life. I've become a finisher. My yes is a yes. I follow through. My family, my friends, my world and now my ministry are beneficiaries of the stability that God has worked in my life.

More importantly, I've learned this about our God. We can depend on Him for the divine yes. Through His word, he has given us a divine yes in all things concerning life, death and throughout eternity. If it's salvation from trouble, you have a yes. Maybe, it's healing in your body, through Christ Jesus, God said yes!

Many live in poverty; because they don't know God said yes to prosperity that overrides the curse of poverty in their life. Or perhaps, you're like I was, unstable with lots of maybes and yeses that turned out to be nos. God intervened in my life with His divine yes. He settled me and made me firm in Christ.

I used to bring up all the reasons, I was so unstable. Like all the bad things that happened to me that made me this way. One day, I dropped all the excuses; I mean reasons; I took responsibility for my sins, my short comings and said, "God help me.

I confess, I've been like water and the wind, turning whichever way my circumstances turned me. I've been unable to change myself, help me..." Then came the word of prophecy. The rest is history.

**21 Days To Destiny Challenge Exercise** (Memorize Memory Scripture, Pray and Say it aloud throughout every day of the challenge.)

**Memory Scripture:** For we are God's workmanship, created in Christ Jesus to do good works, which God prepared in advance for us to do. (Eph. 2:10).

**Confession:** I am a woman of destiny, prepared in advance to do good works

_____

_____

_____

# Day 19: Powers Of Destiny

*WOW Word of Today: The day is almost ended, we must quickly fulfill our God given task for night is coming when no man can work. John 12:13*

Now, the question becomes, how can I be more effective in fulfilling my destiny? I have listed twelve energies that will continue to move us forward in fulfilling our destiny and dreams, successfully:

The power of urgency. Get a sense of urgency about fulfilling your passion, purpose and power in God. Know that we are as a shuttle flying through the night. Number your days aright. The writer of John said, "The day is almost ended, we must quickly fulfill our God given task for night is coming when no man can work." John 12:13

The power of love. We are as loud clanging cymbal, if we do not love. Love with the love of Christ, the Agape love. As you fulfil your destiny, in love, you grow fruit that remains. Fruit that our Lord Jesus can be proud of and announce to the world.

The power of forgiveness. A life full of the passion, purpose and power of God is a life unhindered, walking in forgiveness. Whatever you forgive, Father God forgives and whatever you retain, he retains.

**21 Days To Destiny Challenge Exercise** (Memorize Memory Scripture, Pray and Say it aloud throughout every day of the challenge.)

**Memory Scripture:** For we are God's workmanship, created in Christ Jesus to do good works, which God prepared in advance for us to do. (Eph. 2:10).

**Confession:** I am a woman of destiny, prepared in advance to do good works

_____

_____

_____

# Day 20: Decide And Act

*WOW Word of Today: So you see, faith by itself isn't enough. Unless it produces good deeds, it is dead and useless. -James 2:17*

Here are six questions to ask yourself, periodically. It will keep you moving forward in Christ, pursuing your destiny, increasing in faith to faith and glory to glory.

The first three are decisions and the last three are actions to confirm your decisions.

1. Do I need to change my perspective?
2. Do I expect to know and walk in my purpose and destiny?
3. Do I believe that God has a plan and wants greater for me?
4. Do I seek the kingdom of God first?
5. Have I asked God for my appointment?
6. Do I renew my mind with the Word of God?

**21 Days To Destiny Challenge Exercise** (Memorize Memory Scripture, Pray and Say it aloud throughout every day of the challenge.)

**Memory Scripture:** For we are God's workmanship, created in Christ Jesus to do good works, which God prepared in advance for us to do. (Eph. 2:10).

**Confession:** I am a woman of destiny, prepared in advance to do good works

# Day 21: Driving Force To Continue

*WOW Word of Today: if indeed you continue in the faith, stable and steadfast, not shifting from the hope of the gospel that you heard, which has been proclaimed in all creation under heaven, and of which I, Paul, became a minister. -Colossians 1:23*

Today, I encourage you to continue in faith and producing the fruit of righteousness. Congratulations on getting started pursuing your destiny through service. Now you must continue to the end. Finishing is even better than starting. Here's one thing that will help you finish strong in the kingdom of God.

Remember, all Scripture is inspired by God and is useful to teach us what is true and to make us realize what is wrong in our lives. It corrects us when we are wrong and teaches us to do what is right. With that in mind, let me tell you briefly about my experience with the Holy Spirit teaching me this principle.

In my beginning days as a Christian, I dreamed a dream that taught me the importance of the word of God in our life. I dreamed I was in a house looking out through a window. I saw a dark, dark tornado storm approaching, headed for my house. I began doing all the things I heard you should do in a storm. I spoke the name of Jesus, repeating it about ten to twenty times.

I bowed my head and stood still for a moment, remembering the 'stand still and see the salvation of the Lord.' I stood with my hands lifted up in loud praise for a few minutes...

Still in the dream, I did all of this while watching this storm approach closer and closer, until it was upon me. It destroyed my house and me in it...I woke up and said that's not scriptural, the righteous aren't destroyed in a storm.

The Holy Spirit immediately said, "Oh but it will be, if you don't do what I've been leading you to do, get in the Word."

I instantly knew what He was talking about. You see for weeks even months, he had been leading me, prompting me, even wooing me to daily start reading the word of God.

I would not take it that seriously, always putting it off. For sure, I never got around to. The rest is history. I started that afternoon and never looked back.

**21 Days To Destiny Challenge Exercise** (Memorize Memory Scripture, Pray and Say it aloud throughout every day of the challenge.)

**Memory Scripture:** For we are God's workmanship, created in Christ Jesus to do good works, which God prepared in advance for us to do. (Eph. 2:10).

**Confession:** I am a woman of destiny, prepared in advance to do good works

_____

_____

_____

_____

# About Author

Farma Brown, twelve book Christian Author and Bible teacher inspires women around the world to become women of destiny, purpose, and victory through speaking engagements, books, and Bible studies. She is also the author of WOW! Women of Worth, WOW! Women of Destiny, WOW! Women of Legacy and numerous other books. She and her husband Varn live in Dallas Texas.

# *Join the WOW! Women Movement!*

Other WOW! Women Books & Resources

**WOW! Women of Worth (Book 1)**
Have you feared you would never know why you are here? If so, you are not alone a Gallup poll has determined that one of people's greatest fears is to die having lived a meaningless life. With passion and grace, author Earma Brown declares there's no better place to look for answers than the Bible. She uncovers a biblical trail of seven strategies to becoming an extraordinary woman using ordinary tools. Her book Women of Worth will help you live a life full of meaning while understanding how to:

- Avoid the mistakes forever caused by low self-esteem.
- Overcome an enemy called insignificance.
- Defeat the dream assassins sent to kill your spirit and your dreams.
- Unlock the potential that many never tap into.
- Gain a sense of destiny that will change your life.

The Desire for a Bright Future! "Father God has put in each of us as a seed, the desire for a bright future," explains Earma. "I have designed the book to hopefully position the reader to receive God's plans to satisfy that longing," Start your journey today using the 7 strategies in everything you do and experience the joy of becoming an extraordinary woman using ordinary tools.

(6x9 paperback)

**WOW! Women of Destiny (Book 2)**
*Discover Purpose that Gives You the Power to Go to Your Destiny!*

Are you fulfilling your purpose? Have you turned your troubles into triumph? Are you a woman of God's destiny and power? With passion, grace and biblical integrity, Earma Brown lays out a map to God's destiny and purpose for women. WOW! Women of Destiny book 2 of the WOW! Women Series is filled with insightful encouragement for women pursuing God's destiny and purpose for their lives. Inside WOW! Women of Destiny you will discover how to:

- Seek God's presence not just the gift and receive patience with the process.
- Develop a spirit of readiness to seize all your opportunities when they come.
- Fuel your passion with your troubles
- Discover passion that points to God's purpose
- Stop the Destiny thieves sent to kill your Dreams and Receive God ordained purpose that leads to power
- Prepare a plan that leaves a legacy in women from generation to generation?

WOW! Women of Destiny is an inspiring celebration of women and men from modern times and history who took or are laying hold of their destiny and making a difference in their family, church, community and world.

The author's personal experiences, cemented with biblical scripture will encourage you to overcome modern day challenges in the church, in society, as well as balancing God's call to destiny through victorious home life and community.

Down to earth and inspiring, WOW! Women of Destiny book two of the WOW! Women book series is not only for women's groups. This book is a must read for Christian men and women alike seeking to empower their wives, sisters, mothers and daughters to fulfill their passion, purpose and power, even their destiny in God's Kingdom.
(6x9 paperback)

**WOW! Women of Legacy (Book 3)**
*7 Ways to Live Your Legacy*

Are you designing your life as a torch? Your eye is on the next generation. Your heart is tune with God. You desire to see the next generation do even better than this one. There's good news! You can live a life of legacy. God is a god of the generations. He is the same yesterday, today and forever. Through God's plan, this generation prepares and passes the torch to the next. Inside this book you will discover seven steps to prepare and live your life as a legacy:

1. Discover A Woman's Pattern Of Power and learn to leave a legacy for generations to come.

2. Uncover A Woman's Royal Call To Rule and tap into your inner queen.

3. Engage In A Woman's War With Words And Break the generational curses threatening to destroy your family.

4. Find A Woman's Will To Win And Overcome the Giants of Your Generation

5. Form A Woman's Torch Of Legacy And prepare the torch of your life.

6. Live A Woman's Life Well and Live the Legacy

7. What's Next: THRIVE, a discipleship and mentoring program for WOW! Women all over the world.

"Father God desires the same for each generation. He has put in each of us a blueprint, the thoughts, plans and desire for a bright future," explains Earma. "I have designed the WOW! Women of Legacy book to hopefully position the reader to receive God's plans, live it and pass it to the next generation," Start your journey today using the seven lessons in everything you do and experience the joy of designing your life, as a torch full of passion, purpose and legacy in God.

Practical and inspiring, WOW! Women of Destiny book three of the WOW Women Book Series is not only for women's groups. This book is a must read for Christian men and women alike seeking to empower their wives, sisters, mothers and daughters to fulfill their passion, purpose, power, and live their life as a legacy.

(6x9 paperback)

For an opportunity to get all the WOW! Women books and resources at once, visit Earma at the WOW! Women Shop http://wowontheweb.com/shop/

### Other WOW! Women Workbooks & Resources

- WOW! Women of Worth Devotional 21 Day WORD Challenge (6x9 paperback)
- WOW! Women of Destiny Devotional & 21 Days To Destiny Challenge (6x9 paperback)
- WOW! Women of Legacy Devotional & 21 Days of Blessings and Prayer Challenge (6x9 paperback)
- WOW! Women of Worth Workbook (7x10 paperback)
- WOW! Women of Destiny Workbook (7x10 paperback)
- WOW! Women of Legacy Workbook (7x10 paperback)

**WOW! Women Trilogy Gift Collection**

**WOW! Women Resource Websites**

**WOW! Women On The Web**
- Filled with free and fun stuff
- WOW! Women Blog
- Free Sample Chapters
- Free Discussion Guides
- Book Club

http://www.wowontheweb.com

**WOW! Women Shop**
WOW! Women Books
WOW! Women Workbooks
WOW! Women Products
http://wowontheweb.com/shop/

**WOW! Women Global Membership**
Join the WOW! Women Movement and community. Access all WOW! Women books, leader guides, study and discussion guides, challenge planners (downloadable, printable) and more. Become a member and receive 30% off WOW! Women merchandise and complementary products. Go there now for introductory offer, while it lasts.

http://www.wowwomenglobal.com

Notes:

Notes:

_____

*Notes:*

*Notes:*

*Notes:*

Made in the USA
Columbia, SC
11 September 2024